T0067891

GOD'S GRACIOUS GLORY

A Book of Poetry and Photography

JEAN MARIE PATTY

authorHOUSE®

AuthorHouse™
1663 Liberty Drive
Bloomington, IN 47403
www.authorhouse.com
Phone: 833-262-8899

Published by AuthorHouse 11/04/2022

ISBN: 978-1-6655-7543-0 (sc)
ISBN: 978-1-6655-7542-3 (e)

Contents

Acknowledgements

This book is dedicated to the loving memory of my precious
mother-in-law, Mary Patty, whom I love and miss greatly!
I give all my glory to God above for He is the
Creator of all that is sacred and wonderful!
I love you with all my heart and soul! Thank
you for your many gifts and blessings!
I would like to thank my loving husband and very
best friend, Mark, who is supportive of all that
I create. I love you with all of my being!
Thanks to my sister and brother and their
children...you all mean the world to me.
A very special thanks goes to my beautiful friend, Jennifer
A. Holt, who inspired me to write a second book. She has
been instrumental in so much of my healing recently.
Many thanks go to my dear friend, Donna Goray,
whose love for Christ and all things creative truly
inspires me! Thanks to her sweet children as well.
A warm thanks to my friend, Ann-Marie Cochran, whom I
love and adore. Your faith and love are an inspiration to me!

Next, I would like to thank a few very special friends who have given me love and support for many years, these include: Nancie C. Chapman, Lynn Stanley, Rosemary Hollingsworth, Sara Marie & Joe Lombardo, Libby & Pat Ward, Michele Morgan, Frances Carr, Jim Wilson, Debbie Young, Kelli Craddock Terry, Myra & Bill Snow, Judith Keat, Edith Hysell, Barry Thompson, Susan Tankersley and Brandy Almeida. Thanks to all my other friends who love life and Jesus...you know who you are! Last, but not least, a very special thanks goes to my publisher, AuthorHouse! Thanks for helping me create this work that is so special to me!

Amazing Nature

The sun was beating
down upon my face.
I could feel its beauty
and God's ever present grace.

The leaves were gently
falling to the ground.
I like the way they feel
They make a magical sound.

The cats were walking
all around the trees.
There wasn't a sound
Just the whisper of the breeze.

The trees are so mighty
The clouds are amazing.
I love the beautiful flowers
I just sit there gazing.

Jean Marie Patty

Ann-Marie and Kelsey

She lost her daughter
six years ago.
She was very sad
and couldn't let it go.

Now Ann-Marie is grateful
for the time they shared.
She loves her sweet Kelsey
and they both always cared.

They cared for each other
and had a great time.
Now Kelsey is in Heaven
and she is feeling sublime.

Ann-Marie is happy
but still she gets sad.
She misses her Kelsey
but also she is glad.

She is glad that Kelsey
reigns in Heaven above.
Kelsey is still beautiful
She is filled with perfect love!

Jean Marie Patty

Killdeer

Awesome Ann-Marie

Ann-Marie is ever so sweet
and also she is kind.
She never speaks an ill word
of those she leaves behind.

She and I love to talk of Jesus
and all that He has done.
We love His many creations
and we have so much fun.

We talk about our families
and all the things we love.
We talk about our pets
that were sent from above.

I love Ann-Marie
with all of my heart.
She is so very dear
We are never far apart.

Jean Marie Patty

Believe in the Lord

The Lord will set you free
if only you believe.
For He is full of love
and reigns in Heaven above.

The Lord blesses all who care
and He will always be there.
So lift your spirits high
and you will never sigh.

The Lord is holy
and He is pure.
I love Him so much
and that is for sure.

Jean Marie Patty

Gorgeous Girls

Bree Angel

Bree, you are an angel
Sent from up above.
You make me happy and
You show me sweet love.

Bree, you are so pretty
And lovely as can be.
You are the greatest kitty
You fill my heart with glee.

Bree, you lie on my chest
And make me feel sublime.
I'm so glad I found you
I'm so glad you are mine.

Jean Marie Patty

Cream Puff (Wee One)

Cream Puff, I love you so
I'll never let you go.
You mean so much to me
that's all I need to know.

Cream Puff was sent to me
from Heaven up above.
She is so beautiful
and she fills my heart with love.

Jesus made all the babies
They are so very sweet.
I love all of them
They are wonderfully neat.

My Cream Puff is called
a little wee one.
She loves to play
and soak in the sun.

Jean Marie Patty

Cream Puff Wee One

Dear Donna

Donna is my sweet friend
She is so very kind.
She taught me to paint
and is always on my mind.

Donna loves the Lord
and loves her children too.
She lives her life in peace
She is so very true.

Donna makes me happy
We love to talk and such.
She means the world to me
I love her so very much.

Jean Marie Patty

Dearest Jewel

Dear sweet Jewel
She is a close friend.
Dear kind Jewel
I love her to the end.

Jewel is very special
She listens with loving care.
We have so much in common
Our bond is what we share.

Jewel is humble
And has a gentle spirit.
My life would be lonely
If Jewel were not in it.

Dear sweet Jewel is funny
She always makes me laugh.
Jewel believes in God above
She keeps me on the right path.

Jean Marie Patty

Fanciful Flowers

Dear Mom

I know you are in Heaven
And I know you hear me too.
Please know always that
My love for you is true.

I miss you so much
I don't know what to do.
I cry and I cry
And I often feel so blue.

I know this time will pass
And I'll have things to do.
But while I'm feeling lonely
I know you'll guide me through.

Jean Marie Patty

Dear Sweet Dad

Dear Dad, I love you so.
You made me so proud.
Dad, you are everything
I sing your praises out loud.

My dear sweet Dad,
I miss you so much.
You were so sweet
We loved to talk and such.

Dad, I know you're in Heaven
With the angels above.
You are with Mom too
You fill my heart with love.

You made me so happy.
I don't know what to do.
Even though you're not here
I'll love you forever so true.

Jean Marie Patty

Rock wall

Feathers From Heaven

Feathers are sent to
us from above.
They fall from angel wings
and they represent love.

Feathers are important
To me because…
I had a cat named Feather
And perfect she was.

She was fluffy, sweet
And oh so neat.
Just like an angel
She knocked me off my feet.

So when I find a feather
I keep it close to me.
It represents a special girl
Who fills my heart with glee.

Jean Marie Patty

God Is Everywhere

Lord of Lords and
King of Kings...
You are the maker
of every living thing.

You made the bunnies
They're oh so sweet.
You made the flowers
They're oh so neat.

God made the animals
large and small.
He made the people
wonderful and all.

God sent His son
to set us free.
This is what I
shall always believe.

Jean Marie Patty

Lake Yahou

God Is Forgiving

God is a mighty God
I pray without ceasing.
He is an awesome God
I won't stop believing!

God is kind to all
He is wonderful.
God's love is everlasting
and He is beautiful!

God loves everyone
but not everything we do.
He is a forgiving God
I love Him through and through!

God made the trees
And the ocean too.
God made everything
He is always true!

Jean Marie Patty

God's Precious Jewel

You are a precious Jewel
I know this to be true.
You make me feel happy
Even when you are blue.

The times we spend together
Mean so much to me.
I enjoy our conversations
Jewel fills my heart with glee.

We love to ponder life
And all the beauty in it.
We choose to count our blessings
And pray to the Holy Spirit.

Jewel and I get together
And talk about God.
We think He is awesome
While some may think it's odd.

Jewel holds a special place
In my soul and heart.
Together we make memories
We are never far apart.

Jean Marie Patty

Mexican Petunias

Gracious And Good

You make everything right, Lord
You make everything real.
You make everything right, Lord
You make me want to feel.

You are gracious and good
You make all things right.
You are wonderful to me
and you're here day and night.

I love you all the time
and you give so much to me.
You are kind and merciful
and you love every living thing.

Jean Marie Patty

Happy Mother's Day, Mom

The sweet, short and precious life
of our beloved Polly had to come
to an end, but she is not really far away.
She lives on in our hearts forever.
She is remembered and loved by many.
She lives in God's kingdom forever.
Polly is precious to all of us.
She was a wonderful wife and mother,
daughter and grandmother, sister and friend.
Her memory will reign forever
and she will never be forgotten.
She will always be young and beautiful.
She is now safe in the arms of Jesus.
She is safe from all harm and
sickness.
We love and miss you, Polly!
You are beautiful to all of us!
We love you forever!

Have a great time in Heaven and
we will be thinking about you today
and every single day!

Jean Marie Patty

Fancy Feline

Heavenly Judith

I love sweet Judith
She is kind as can be.
She lost her beautiful Amy
But finally she can see.

She can see that God
is awesome and glorious.
He watches over us and
helps us remain victorious.

Judith never loses hope
and believes in God above.
She is good to everyone
She is sweeter than a dove.

Judith will surely see
her precious angel one day.
They are both heavenly
and for them I always pray.

Jean Marie Patty

His Love Is A Gift

Look at our lovely tulips
God's magnificent creation.
He is an awesome power
Full of mighty jubilation!

God made all things
Great and small.
He is full of love
He is forever all!

God's love is a gift
Sent from up above.
He is the greatest and
He made the sweetest dove!

God made everyone and
He loves us so much.
He fills our life with beauty
And His precious gentle touch!

Jean Marie Patty

Awesome Angel

I Love God

My God is real
That is how I feel.
Our God is love
He reigns up above.

God gives me strength
and guides me through.
He answers my prayers
He is wonderful too.

God is the sunshine
and the morning dew.
He loves the children
The animals and you.

God is a wave
That crashes so high.
God is a butterfly
that soars across the sky.

We all need God
every single day.
I do love God
more than I can say.

Jean Marie Patty

I Love The Lord

I love the Lord
For He is gracious.
I love the Lord
I give my heart to Him!

I love the Lord
For He is courageous.
I love the Lord
For He is kind!

I love the Lord
For He is wonderful.
I love the Lord
He is my best friend!

Jean Marie Patty

Sensational Sunset

Jesus Is Merciful

Jesus, you are kind and good
You are merciful too.
Jesus, you are everything
You are ever so true!

Jesus, you are sweet
I'm so happy you came.
You fill my life with blessings
I love to praise your name!

God gave us a gift
When He sent you.
He gave us everlasting love
And sweet forgiveness too!

God made all people
And the animals too.
He gave us the flowers
And the sky so blue!

Jean Marie Patty

Jesus is Real

You give me joy everyday
You show me love in every way.
I love you so
and that is all I know.

Jesus is real
and oh so divine.
He makes everything right
and He is always mine.

I love sweet Jesus
with all of my heart.
He is truly love
We are never far apart.

Jean Marie Patty

Honey Bee

Jesus, You Are Beautiful

Jesus, you are so sweet
You make all things right.
You are so loving
Through every day and night.

Thank you for your kindness
And your forgiveness too.
You make me so faithful
And you make me so true.

Jesus, you are the only one
Who can help me to live right.
You help me to want to give
And I want to live this life.

You are so kind and
You are beautiful.
You are God's only son
And you are dutiful.

Jean Marie Patty

Jovial Jeanette

Jeanette was a fine lady
and was ever so kind.
She was truly funny
and always spoke her mind.

Mamaw was sent to us
from God up above.
She filled us with joy
and gave us great love.

We will all miss Jeanette
but she's not really gone.
She lives on forever and
we praise her in song.

The angels guide Mamaw
and keep her safe.
She lives in harmony and
she's in a perfect place.

Jean Marie Patty

Delicate Daisies

Joyful Jennifer

I love my friend, Jennifer
She is so very kind.
She loves life and God
She is a wonderful find!

Jennifer sees beauty
in all of God's creations.
We love to share stories
about life and jubilation's!

Jennifer has helped me so much
to deal with my grief.
She speaks words of wisdom
and provides a sense of relief!

I love Jennifer so much
She is a beautiful friend.
She is always courageous
I will love her to the end!

Jean Marie Patty

Life

Life is love
Love is truth.
Why do we always
Miss our youth?

We start out small
Then grow so fast.
We leave a trail
Far from our past.

We start to look back
Over the years…
Then lose our loved ones
And fight back the tears.

Finally there is joy again
And we continue to live.
We struggle through life
And we hope and forgive.

Jean Marie Patty

Curious Cat

Live For Each Moment

Some people like to read
and others like to pray.
Whatever is your pleasure
try to do it every day.

Children like to play
and some adults do too.
It's fun to laugh and talk
but sometimes we feel blue.

When you're feeling down
Try to think of the good.
Be kind to others
and do what you should.

There is only so much time
to live on this great earth.
So live for each moment
and never forget your worth.

Jean Marie Patty

Missing Bailey

Bailey, I miss you,
But you are doing fine.
You are in Heaven
And you're feeling sublime!

Bailey, I think about you
All of the time.
I know you are well
I'm glad you were mine!

I love you forever, Bailey
You're with Jesus above.
I miss you like crazy
My heart is full of love!

You were the sweetest
dog that ever lived.
I will always think of you
You were the greatest gift!

Jean Marie Patty

Beautiful Bailey Boy

Missing Feather

I love you Feather
Much more than life.
Having you gone is
causing such strife.

My heart is broken
I'm going insane.
I love you forever
I can't stand the pain.

I miss you so much
I don't know what to do.
I cry all the time
I wish I could see you.

Please return safely
And don't be gone long.
I'm dying inside but
I'm trying to be strong.

Jean Marie Patty

My Cat Cream Puff

My sweet Cream Puff
I love you so.
You are special
That's all I know.

You make me smile
You mean so much to me.
Your love is unconditional
You fill my heart with glee.

The cute things you do
make me feel so fine.
Your love is true
You make me feel sublime.

Jean Marie Patty

Fluffy Feather

My Loving Brother

My brother is so funny
That is what I know.
He loves his mom and dad
and he loves to let it show.

My brother likes my poetry
For this I am so grateful.
He is always kind
and he is never hateful.

He loves his daughter
and that is for sure.
She is so beautiful
His love for her is pure.

Jean Marie Patty

My Loving Parents

My loving Mom and Dad
mean so much to me.
I love them both dearly
They fill my heart with glee.

My ever caring parents
love me very much.
I cherish them daily
We like to talk and such.

My parents are truly angels
They protect and they guide.
They always watch over me
and never leave my side.

My Mom and Dad
are special and kind.
I love them so much
They're in my heart and mind.

Jean Marie Patty

New Hampshire Blues

My Precious Mary

My dear precious Mary
was everything to me.
I love her more than life
and that you can believe.

She was always nurturing
and so very kind.
She was truly an angel
She is always on my mind.

My Mom would talk with me
and help me to see
that life is not always fair
but it can set us free.

I love my sweet Mary
with all of my being.
She was precious and dear
and always worth seeing.

Jean Marie Patty

My Sweet Emme Dog

I love you Emme
for you are mine.
I love you Emme
until the end of time.

I love you Emme
for you are true.
You are beautiful
and I love you!

You are sweet
and you are kind.
You are loved
and a wonderful find!

Jean Marie Patty

Extraordinary Emme

My Sweet Mom

It's been over a year
But it's still vivid in my mind.
Mom was the sweetest person
She was so special and kind.

I miss her so much
I love her to the end.
She is my sweet Mom
She was my special friend.

I wish I could talk to Mom
I long to see her face.
She was everything to me
She was filled with such grace.

I think about you often
And miss you so much.
You're always in my thoughts.
I keep our memories and such.

Jean Marie Patty

My Sweet Sister

For my sweet sister
whom I love and adore.
She is so very special
and that I can't ignore.

We tell each other secrets
and that is what we share.
We love to talk so much
and she'll always be there.

I love my sister
with all of my heart.
She is very dear to me
From her I cannot part.

Jean Marie Patty

Meredith NH

Nostalgic Nancie

Nancie is my very dear friend
She is always nice to me.
She sends me beautiful letters
And they help me feel so free.

Nancie loves the sweet Lord
And she adores her family.
She sends me gorgeous photos
And they fill my heart with glee.

Nancie and I go way back
She has always been my friend.
We share such fond memories
And I will love her to the end.

Jean Marie Patty

Our Dear Lord

The Lord is good
all of the time.
I love Him so much
Forever He is mine!

The Lord is mighty
and He is proud.
I sing His praises
We sing them our loud!

The Lord hears everyone
and knows our needs.
He always cares for us
and He never leaves!

Jean Marie Patty

Whispering Willow

Our Lord Is Kind

The Lord is near
and He is here.
He is gracious
and He is dear.

Our Lord shows favor
to all who care.
Our Lord is forgiving
and He is everywhere.

The Lord is wonderful
and He is kind.
He is merciful
and He is divine.

Jean Marie Patty

Precious Hannah

Dear sweet Hannah
You know I love you so.
You are a special girl
My heart won't let you go.

I know you are in Heaven
where the sky is always blue.
I love you forever
You are so very true.

Hannah, you were sweet
and I will always care.
One day I hope to see you
I would like to make it there.

I pray that you are
with my mom and dad.
I hope you are with Emme
but I'm still a little sad.

Jean Marie Patty

Peeking Puff

Radiant Rosemary

Rosemary is my dear friend
She is so very sweet.
She likes to draw and paint
She is a special treat.

Rosemary really loves animals
She is so very kind.
She loves her family and friends
She knows the ties that bind.

Rosemary is very talented
She is someone to adore.
She lives for the Lord
and that I can't ignore.

Jean Marie Patty

So Kind

Just look at you
Your love is true.
What in the world
Is a girl to do?

She would die
without his love.
She loves him so
He was sent from above.

You are funny
And oh so kind.
You are special to
my heart and my mind.

Jean Marie Patty

Radiant Rose

Something Greater

Where do you go
when you're all alone?
Is it deep inside your mind
or is it far from home?

Have you ever been so lonely
you thought that you would die?
Did you ever feel so empty
That all you could do was cry?

Whenever you find yourself
feeling these emotions...
This is what you do
Let go of the commotions.

For something in this world
is far greater than we are.
He can answer all your prayers
He's in the twinkle of a star.

Jean Marie Patty

Sweet Charles

I only knew you
for a short while.
But in that time
you always made me smile.

You were so sweet
and so very kind.
I grew to love you
You're in my heart and mind.

Your sweet Fran loves you
This I know to be true.
You're in the arms of Jesus
where the sky is always blue.

You will suffer no more
and feel no sadness.
I am happy for you
You will only find gladness.

Jean Marie Patty

Cute Cotton

Sweet Frannie

Fran is my dear friend
I love her 'til the end.
She is so very kind
She is a wonderful find.

Frannie is so special
She means the world to me.
We both love our babies
and that you can believe.

We love to talk and share
and she knows that I care.
We spend a lot of time
and we get along just fine.

I love Frannie more each day
We love to chat and pray.
Fran is everything to me
She fills my heart with glee.

Jean Marie Patty

The Greatest Dog

Bailey, you are sweet
and ever so kind.
You fill up my days,
my heart and my mind!

Bailey, you are so true
You mean the world to me.
I love you forever
Special is how you'll always be!

You are the greatest dog
in the whole wide land.
I love you so much
You make me feel so grand!

Bailey, you are so cute
I love your sweet eyes.
You are ever so beautiful
and a wonderful surprise!

Jean Marie Patty

Delightful Dogwood

The Lord is Here

We all must suffer
That is just the way.
We all feel pain
through every single day.

God gives us strength
to make it through
He gives us grace
and many blessings too.

Do not be afraid
For the Lord is here.
He makes us feel better
He is so very dear.

God's love is beautiful
He makes life all right.
Let us praise him with joy
through every day and night.

Jean Marie Patty

The Pain of Grief

Sometimes things happen
that cause such grief.
You can't stand the way it feels
You long for some relief.

It's a gut wrenching pain
that eats you up inside.
It's an uneasy feeling
from which you cannot hide.

It's the kind of pain that
makes you feel such dread.
It rips your heart out
then makes you lose your head.

The pain hurts more than ever
You think you'll go insane.
You just want it to stop
but the thoughts are so inane.

Jean Marie Patty

Soft Smokey

You Are Merciful

Save me, I know...
God, you are holy and pure.
I love you with my whole heart
You are the One for sure.

How can you know
How much I love you so?
You are very beautiful
And I'll never let you go.

God, you are merciful
And ever so true.
I love you forever.
You're all I want to pursue.

Jean Marie Patty

You Are The Living Light

I love you so much, Lord
You are my reason for living.
I worship only you, Lord
You make me feel like giving.

You are the one and only
You are the most High.
You make me happy and
I'll see you when I die.

I love you forever, Lord
You are the living light.
You are the greatest one
You make everything right.

Jean Marie Patty

Pretty Puff

Printed in the United States
by Baker & Taylor Publisher Services